The Coats Book of
MODERN EUROPEAN
EMBROIDERY

CONTENTS

Modern European Embroidery

There was an era when the country of origin of a piece of embroidery could be identified with ease. Foremost in this analysis was the design and secondly the stitches used. Today, identification is much more difficult. The leading designers of all crafts, including embroidery, travel widely and naturally they are influenced by what they see in other lands. However, in many instances they are still controlled by their traditional stitch techniques.

This book contains a comprehensive collection of modern European embroidery which includes some designs based mainly on traditional work and others, which have been influenced by modern trends.

General instructions

Metric measurements

As designers are now working in the metric system, it is only possible to provide pattern instructions with complete accuracy in metric measurements. In this book we give approximate imperial measurement equivalents in brackets after the metric size where we feel they are still useful, ie in setting out fabric widths in the materials required, but in detailed working instructions we show only the metric measurements.

For readers who still prefer to work in imperial measurement, a brief comparison guide is given for shorter measurements; for longer measurements, the easiest way to convert is to use a tape measure showing inches and centimetres, but it should be stressed that for best results only the metric measurements should be used.

COMPARISON GUIDE FOR SHORT MEASUREMENTS
(APPROXIMATE)

1 cm =	$\frac{3}{8}$ in.		35 cm =	$13\frac{3}{4}$ in.	
1.5 cm =	$\frac{5}{8}$ in.		40 cm =	$15\frac{3}{4}$ in.	
2 cm =	$\frac{3}{4}$ in.		45 cm =	$17\frac{3}{4}$ in.	
2.5 cm =	1 in.		50 cm =	$19\frac{3}{4}$ in.	
5 cm =	2 in.		55 cm =	$21\frac{5}{8}$ in.	
7.5 cm =	3 in.		60 cm =	$23\frac{5}{8}$ in.	
10 cm =	4 in.		65 cm =	$25\frac{5}{8}$ in.	
12.5 cm =	5 in.		70 cm =	$27\frac{1}{2}$ in.	
15 cm =	6 in.		75 cm =	$29\frac{1}{2}$ in.	
17.5 cm =	$6\frac{7}{8}$ in.		80 cm =	$31\frac{1}{2}$ in.	
20 cm =	$7\frac{7}{8}$ in.		85 cm =	$33\frac{1}{2}$ in.	
22.5 cm =	$8\frac{7}{8}$ in.		90 cm =	$35\frac{1}{2}$ in.	
25 cm =	$9\frac{7}{8}$ in.		95 cm =	$37\frac{3}{8}$ in.	
27.5 cm =	$10\frac{7}{8}$ in.		100 cm =	$39\frac{3}{8}$ in.	
30 cm =	$11\frac{3}{4}$ in.		(1 metre)		

Buying fabrics

LENGTH (APPROXIMATE)

10 cm =	4 in.	60 cm =	$23\frac{5}{8}$ in.
20 cm =	$7\frac{7}{8}$ in.	70 cm =	$27\frac{1}{2}$ in.
30 cm =	$11\frac{3}{4}$ in.	80 cm =	$31\frac{1}{2}$ in.
40 cm =	$15\frac{3}{4}$ in.	90 cm =	$35\frac{1}{2}$ in.
50 cm =	$19\frac{3}{4}$ in.	1 m =	$39\frac{3}{8}$ in.

Tracing methods

This book contains both counted thread and free-style embroidery designs. The former are worked from a chart, but the designs of the latter technique must be transferred to the fabric.

We give four methods of reproducing designs as follows:

1   The simplest method is with the use of carbon paper. Yellow or light blue carbon paper may be used on dark coloured fabric, black or dark blue carbon paper on light coloured fabric. Place the carbon paper in position face downwards on the fabric, then place the drawing or tracing of the design on top. Draw over all the lines with a sharp-pointed pencil. Care must be taken to press only on the lines of the design, otherwise the carbon may smudge the fabric.

2   Trace the design on to firm tracing paper, then with a needle, prick small holes over all the lines, spacing the holes evenly about 2 mm apart. Rub the back of the pricked design with fine sand-paper to remove the roughness. Place the pricked design on to the fabric and keep in position with weights. Rub powdered charcoal (for light coloured fabric) or powdered chalk (for dark coloured fabric) through the holes. Remove the tracing paper and blow off the surplus powder from the fabric. Paint over the dotted lines of powder with water colour paint, using a fine brush and not too much water. Use dark or light coloured paint depending upon the colour of the fabric. Alternatively a fixative spray can be used to fix the powder to the fabric.

3   The design can be traced directly on to fine transparent fabric such as organdie, nylon or fine silk, by placing the design underneath the fabric and painting over the lines with water colour paint or tracing with a soft pencil.

4   The surface on very coarse or textured fabric, may make it difficult to trace or paint a design. In this case, trace the drawing on to fine tracing paper, baste the paper in position on the fabric, then carefully mark over all the lines of the design with small running stitches. The drawing can be torn away before the embroidery is commenced. Remove all basting stitches after the completion of the embroidery.

Embroidery frames

Some embroideries with areas of closely worked stitches are apt to pucker. In this case, an embroidery frame is recommended to help keep the work flat and even. There are several types of frames. An embroidery ring is most commonly used for small pieces of work. The ring usually consists of two wooden or metal rings, fitting closely one within the other, so that the fabric may be stretched tightly. These rings can be obtained in various sizes, the most useful type having a small screw on the larger ring for loosening or tightening it. This allows any thickness of fabric to be used. The section of embroidery to be worked is placed over the smaller of the rings, the other ring being pressed down over the fabric on the smaller ring to hold the work taut. If a screw is attached, this should be tightened. The warp and weft threads of the fabric must be straight in the ring. For large pieces of embroidery, especially tapestries, the work should be mounted on a square or rectangular frame.

Embroidery rings and frames can be supplied with a stand, which leaves the embroiderer's hands free.

Sewing thread recommendation

When making up or finishing articles, use the multi-purpose sewing thread Coats *Drima* (polyester). This thread is fine, yet very strong and is obtainable in a wide range of shades. To help you obtain smooth and secure stitching on your selected fabric, the equivalent fabrics and needles are as follows:

Fine/medium fabrics, eg cotton, linen, canvas — machine needle No. 14 or 16 (British); 90 or 100 (Continental); Number of stitches to the centimetre (inch) 4 - 5 (10 - 12); Milward hand needle No. 6 or 7.

Bias strips

To cut strips on the bias, fold the fabric diagonally so that the lengthwise thread lies parallel to the width-wise thread (diagram 1). When the fabric is pulled on the true bias, it gives the maximum elasticity. Cut strips the desired width and join to form the required length. Diagrams 2 and 3 show the correct method.

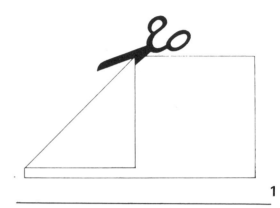

1

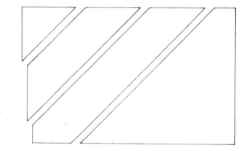

2

3

Marking the centre of fabric

Free style embroidery: when the instructions require the fabric to be folded in half 'both ways' do this in two stages, ie

1 Fold the fabric in half, iron fold and open out.
2 Fold the fabric in half in the opposite direction and iron along the fold. When the fabric is opened out ready for transferring, the centre is immediately seen.

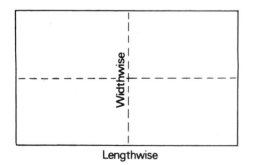

Mitred corner

A mitre is a fold used to achieve smooth shaping at a corner. To mitre a corner of a hem, fold and press the hem; open out the hem and fold the corner inwards on the inner fold line. Cut off the corner, leaving a small seam allowance diagram 1. Refold the hem and slipstitch the diagonal line of the mitre in position diagram 2.

Framing

Place glass (if desired) cardboard mount and embroidery into frame and secure with small panel pins. Paste a sheet of brown paper over the back edge of the frame to seal. Screw in two picture rings approximately one third of the height from the top. Attach a piece of cord to the rings.

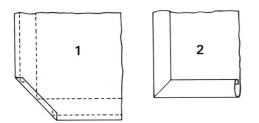

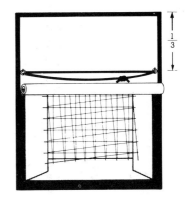

Making-up picture

Place the embroidery centrally over the backing board, fold the surplus fabric to the back and secure at top with pins into the edge of board. Pull firmly over the lower edge and pin in position. Repeat on side edges pulling fabric until it lies taut on the board. Secure at the back by lacing from side to side both ways with a strong thread. Remove pins.

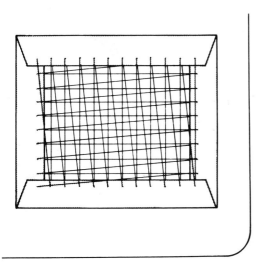

11

Stitches

Back stitch

Bring the thread through on the stitch line, then take a small backward stitch through the fabric. Bring the needle through again a little in front of the first stitch, take another stitch, inserting the needle at the point where it first came through.

Whipped back stitch

Work back stitch first, then with another thread in the needle, whip over each back stitch without entering the fabric.

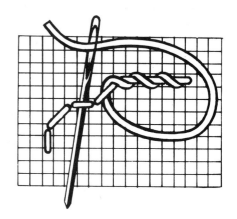

Double back stitch or closed herringbone stitch

This stitch is used for shadow work on fine transparent fabric and can be worked on the right side of the fabric as at A - a small back stitch worked alternately on each side of the traced double lines (the dotted lines on the diagram show the formation of the thread on the wrong side of the fabric). The colour of the thread appears delicately through the fabric. Figure B - shows the stitch worked on the wrong side of the fabric as a closed herringbone stitch with no spaces left between the stitches. Both methods achieve the same result.

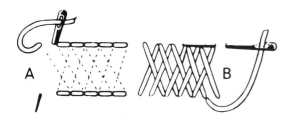

Buttonhole stitch

Figure 1 - bring the thread out on the lower line, insert the needle in position on the upper line, taking a straight downward stitch with the thread under the needle point. Pull up the stitch to form a loop and repeat. Work the stitches close together. Figure 2 - shows the method of working an eyelet where fabric is cut away on the completion of the embroidery.

As this stitch is used in cut-work embroidery it is most important to have the looped edge of the buttonhole stitch to the part of the fabric to be cut away. Use small sharp-pointed scissors and cut from the wrong side taking care not to snip the stitches.

Chain stitch and chain stitch filling

Bring the thread out at the top of line and hold down with left thumb. Insert the needle where it last emerged and bring the point out a short distance away. Pull the thread through keeping the working thread under the needle point. This stitch can also be used as a filling, rows of chain stitch worked close together within a shape until it is filled completely.

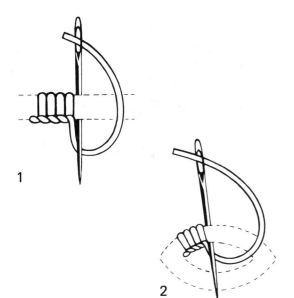

Cable chain stitch

Bring the thread through at A and hold it down with the left thumb. Pass the needle from right to left under the working thread, then twist the needle back over the working thread to the right and, still keeping the thread under the thumb, take a stitch of the required length. Pull thread through.

13

Cross stitch

Bring the thread out at the lower right and take a diagonal stitch to the left over 2 (or as instructed) threads. Continue to end of row making half crosses. On the return journey, complete the cross as shown. The upper stitches of all crosses should lie in the same direction. The cross stitch may be worked in rows or completed as individual stitches, depending upon the design. On square weave fabric the cross stitch is worked in the same way, but each cross is over one square of fabric.

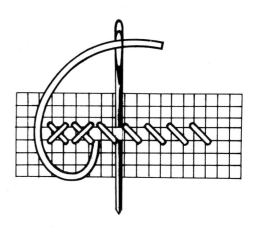

Daisy stitch or detached chain stitch

Work in the same way as chain stitch (A), but fasten each loop at the foot with a small stitch (B). This stitch may be worked singly or in groups to form flower petals.

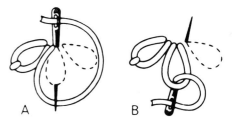

A   B

Double knot stitch

Bring the thread through at A. Take a small stitch across the line at B. Pass the needle downwards under the surface stitch just made, without piercing the fabric, as at C. With the thread under the needle, pass the needle again under the first stitch at D. Pull the thread through to form a knot. The knots should be spaced evenly and closely to obtain a beaded effect.

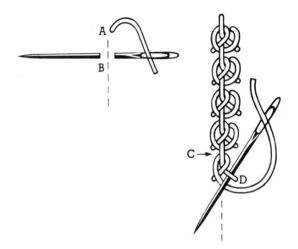

Fly stitch

Bring the thread through at the top left, hold it down with the left thumb, insert the needle to the right on the same level, a little distance from where the thread first emerged and take a small stitch downwards to the centre with the thread below the needle. Pull through and insert the needle again below the stitch at the centre (A) and bring it through in position for the next stitch. This stitch may be worked singly or in horizontal rows (A) or vertically (B).

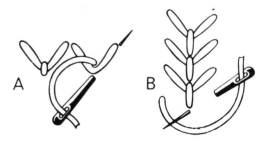

Four-sided stitch

This stitch is worked from right to left. Figure 1 — bring the thread out at A; insert the needle at B (2 threads up), bring out at C (2 threads down and 2 threads to the left); figure 2 — insert at A, bring out at D (2 threads up and 2 threads to the left); figure 3 — insert at B, bring out at C; figure 4 — insert at D to complete a single four-sided stitch. Figure 5 shows a continuous row.

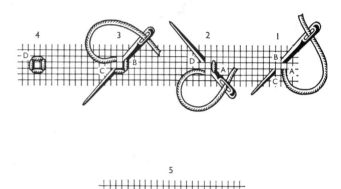

French knots

Bring the thread out at the required position, hold the thread down with the left thumb and encircle the thread twice with the needle, as at A. Still holding the thread firmly, twist the needle back to the starting point and insert it close to where the thread first emerged (see arrow). Pull thread through to the back and secure for a single french knot or pass on to the position of the next stitch as at B.

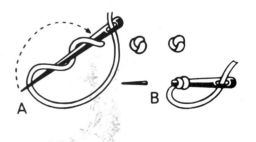

Holbein stitch

Holbein stitch is sometimes called double running stitch. Working from right to left, work a row of running stitch (see this page) over and under required number of threads of fabric, following the shape of the design. On the return journey, work in the same way from left to right, filling in the spaces left in the first row. This stitch is used in Assisi embroidery to outline the cross stitch, but may also be used in other types of designs on evenweave fabric.

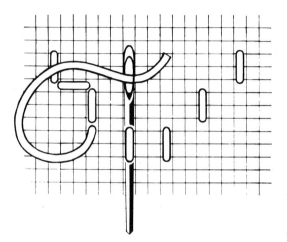

Leaf stitch

Bring the thread through at A and make a sloping stitch to B. Bring the thread through at C and make a sloping stitch to D. Bring the thread through at E, then continue working alternate stitches on each side in this way until the shape is lightly filled. When this stitch is used there is usually an outline of stem stitch or chain stitch worked round the shape.

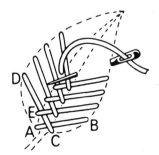

Long and short stitch

This form of satin stitch is so named as all the stitches are of varying lengths. It is often used to fill a shape which is too large or too irregular to be covered by satin stitch. It is also used to achieve a shaded effect. In the first row the stitches are alternately long and short and closely follow the outline of the shape. The stitches in the following rows are worked to achieve a smooth appearance. The diagram shows how a shaded effect may be obtained.

Running stitch

Pass the needle over and under the fabric, making the upper stitches of equal length. The under stitches should also be of equal length, but half the size or less of the upper stitches.

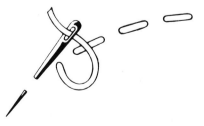

Satin stitch

Proceed with straight stitches worked closely together across the shape, as shown in the diagram. If desired, running stitch or chain stitch may be worked first to form a padding underneath, this gives a raised effect. Care must be taken to keep a good edge. Do not make the stitches too long, as they would then be liable to be pulled out of position.

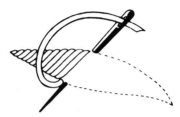

Stem stitch

Work from left to right, taking regular, small stitches along the line of the design. The thread always emerges on the left side of the previous stitch. This stitch is used for flower stems, outlines, etc. It can also be used as a filling, rows of stem stitch worked closely together within a shape until it is filled completely.

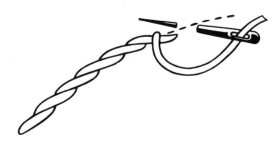

Straight stitch (also known as single satin stitch)

This is shown as single spaced stitches worked either in a regular or irregular manner. Sometimes the stitches are of varying size. The stitches should be neither too long nor too loose. This stitch may also be worked on evenweave fabric.

Wave stitch

This stitch must be worked first, before withdrawing fabric threads. Bring the thread through at A; insert at B (2 threads to the right and 2 threads down), bring through at C (4 threads to the left); insert at A, bring through at D (4 threads to the left). Continue in this way to the end of the row.

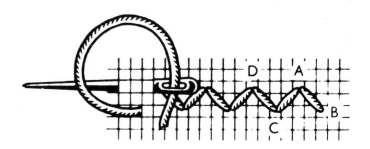

Runner – free style – Germany

In Germany the transition from heavy, though attractive, cross stitch embroidery of a few decades ago, to bold stylised floral and plant motifs is dramatic. This design is an excellent and typical example.

Materials

Clark's Anchor Stranded Cotton: 3 skeins Orange 0326; 2 skeins Jade 0188; 1 skein each Rose Madder 057, Tangerine 0314. Use 4 strands for Double Knot Stitch, 3 strands for remainder of embroidery.

40 cm fine gold embroidery fabric, 115 cm (45 in.) wide.

Milward International Range crewel needles No. 6 and No. 7 for 4 and 3 strands respectively.

Cut fabric 40 x 108 cm and fold the fabric lengthwise and crease lightly. The drawing on page 23 gives one motif, broken line indicates the fold, dotted lines indicate the position of the repeat. With one long side of fabric facing, trace the section as given 7.5 cm from left-hand side. Repeat twice more to the right, spacing as indicated. To complete, turn fabric and trace in same way. Following the diagram on page 24 and number key for the embroidery work section A on the two outer motifs of the design and section B for the centre motif. All parts similar to numbered parts are worked in the same colour and stitch. Press the embroidery on the wrong side. To make up, turn back 1.5 cm hems, mitre corners and stitch.

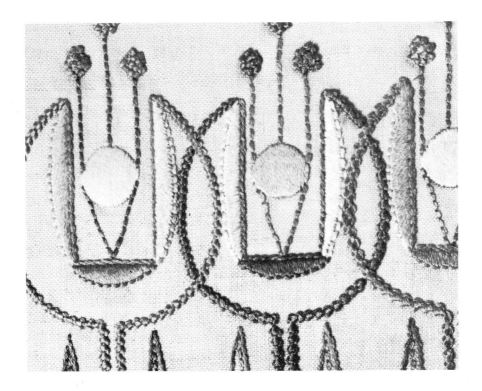

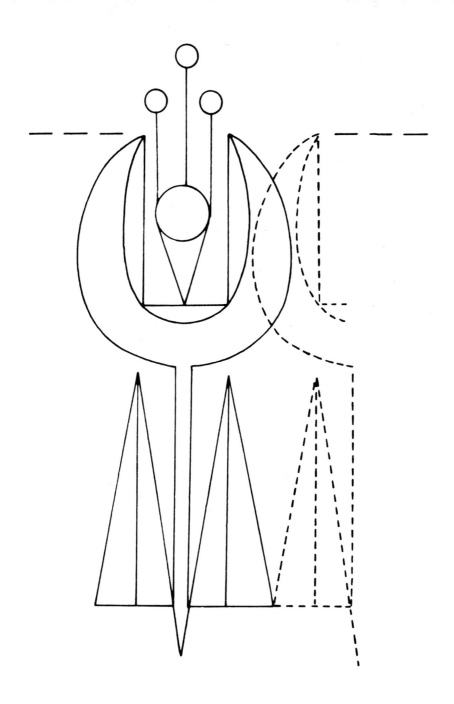

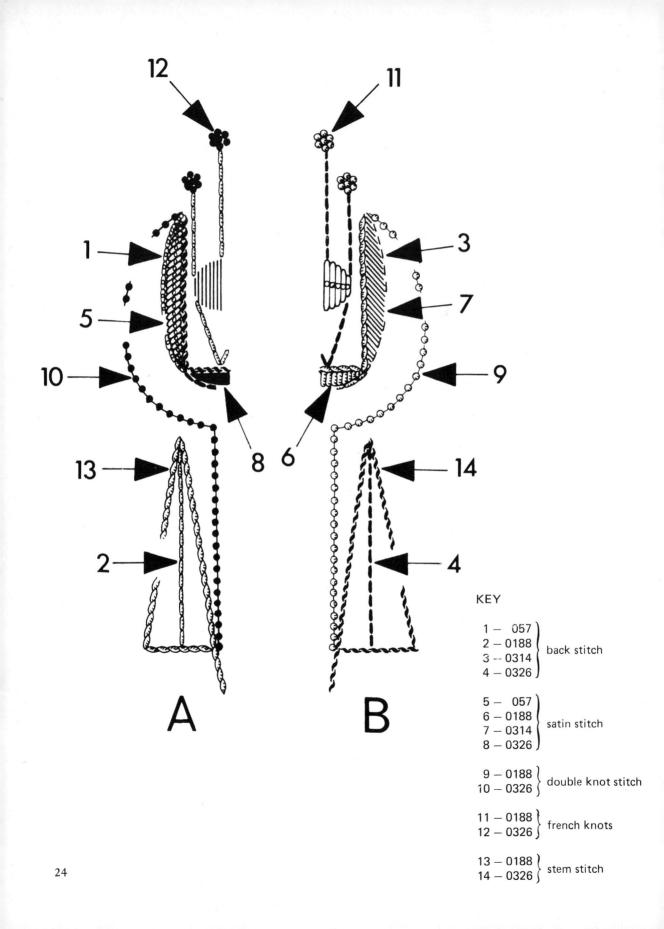

KEY

1 — 057
2 — 0188
3 — 0314
4 — 0326
} back stitch

5 — 057
6 — 0188
7 — 0314
8 — 0326
} satin stitch

9 — 0188
10 — 0326
} double knot stitch

11 — 0188
12 — 0326
} french knots

13 — 0188
14 — 0326
} stem stitch

Plate 1   Tablecloth — Great Britain
working instructions on pages 37—43

*Plate 2   Cushion cover — Great Britain
working instructions on pages 44—46*

Plate 3   Lunch mats — Italy
working instructions on pages 47—49

Plate 4   Lunch mats — Italy
working instructions on pages 50—51

Plate 5   Wall hanging — Finland
          working instructions on pages 52–55

Plate 6   Traycloth — Spain
     working instructions on pages 56—57

Plate 7   *Owl panel — Norway*
           working instructions on pages 60—62

Plate 8   Lampshade — France
working instructions on pages 33—35

Lampshade – cross stitch – France

If you have visited Paris you may have seen the fabulous Can-Can. This embroidered version will provide a souvenir of your visit.

Materials

Clark's Anchor Stranded Cotton: 1 skein each Magenta 065, Old Rose 076, Parma Violet 0112, Jade 0189, Canary Yellow 0288, Terra Cotta 0336, Chestnut 0351 and Black 0403. Use 3 strands throughout.

40 cm pale blue medium weight evenweave fabric, approximately 21 threads to 2.5 cm, 150 cm (59 in.) wide.

40 cm white bonding parchment 102 cm (40 in.) wide or non-adhesive lampshade parchment.

2 lampshade rings 20.3 cm in diameter – one with fitting.

1.40 m matching gimp or braid for edging.

Coats Nainsook bias binding for rings.

1 tube fabric adhesive.

Milward International Range tapestry needle No. 24.

Cut one piece from fabric 29 x 68.5 cm. With one long side facing mark a 20.3 cm square centrally, 7.5 cm from left-hand side, repeat 7.5 cm from right-hand side. Mark the centre of each square both ways with a line of basting stitches. The design is worked over 2 threads of fabric, approximately 10 crosses to 2.5 cm. The diagram on page 35 gives the complete design, centres indicated by blank arrows which should coincide with the basting stitches. Each background square on the diagram represents 2 threads of fabric. With one long side of fabric facing, commence the embroidery centrally and following diagram and sign key work the design within each square. Press the embroidery on the wrong side. To make up. Bind rings tightly overlapping edges of tape. Press 6 mm allowance on long sides of embroidered fabric to wrong side. Cut bonding parchment 28 x 67.2 cm and place on a flat surface shiny side up. Place the wrong side of fabric to parchment with fabric extending 1.5

cm at right-hand side and having left-hand edges even; hold in position with paper clips or weights. Pass a moderately hot iron over fabric to enable the parchment to adhere. Turn back the 1.5 cm margin at right-hand side and stick to parchment with adhesive. Pin fabric-covered parchment in position around rings. Sew securely in place to top ring, starting at unfinished short end and stopping about 5 cm from opposite end; stitch lower ring in position in same way; overlap finished short end and stick in position. If necessary, secure with small stitches using a curved needle. Finish sewing at upper and lower edges. Stitch or stick braid in position.

Note If non-adhesive parchment is used for backing, overlap short ends of parchment to fit rings and glue together. Sew rings to top and lower edges. Baste and stitch short ends of fabric, right sides together to fit over frame. Trim seam if necessary. Turn to right side, pull fabric over frame and sew to rings.

KEY

◙	◳	— 065
◿		— 076
◪		— 0112
◙	◳	— 0189
⊡		— 0288
ⓒ		— 0336
☒		— 0351
■	❏	— 0403

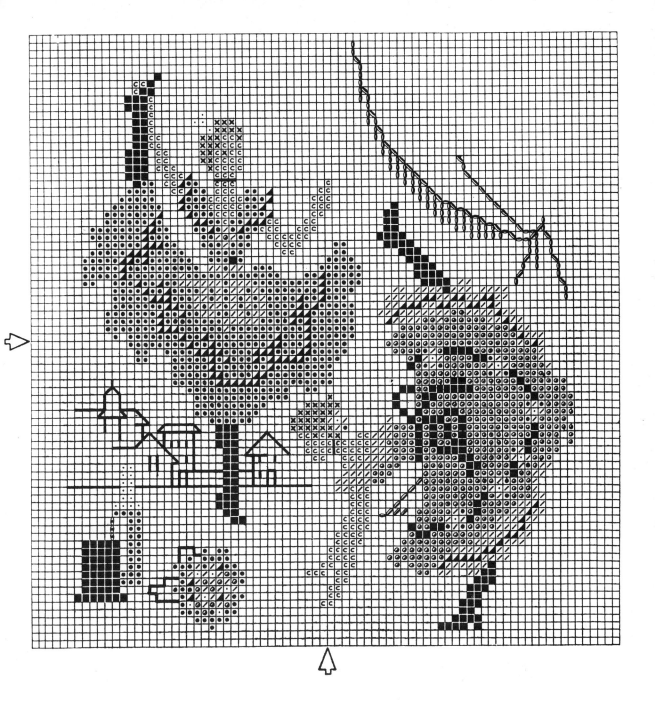

Tablecloth – cross stitch – Great Britain

This tablecloth might be termed a nostalgic collector's piece as it incorporates typical scenes from Scotland, England, Ireland and Wales, all embroidered in the most simple stitch of all — cross stitch. There is no doubt that it would be a most acceptable gift for friends and relatives living overseas.

Materials

Clark's Anchor Stranded Cotton: 5 skeins Black 0403; 1 skein each Cardinal 022, Scarlet 046, Turkey Red 047, Magenta 062, 065, Violet 0100, 0102, Cornflower 0136, 0137, 0139, Forest Green 0218, Almond Green 0261, 0262, 0263, Moss Green 0266, 0269, Muscat Green 0278, 0281, Buttercup 0295, Tangerine 0314, Orange 0323, Flame 0335, Terra Cotta 0336, Peat Brown 0358, Cinnamon 0371, Grey 0400, White 0402, Tapestry Shades 0845, 0888 and 0903. Use 3 strands throughout.

Quantities if required individually — 1 skein of each colour quoted on the appropriate diagram for each country and 4 skeins for the border.

1.50 m white or natural medium weight evenweave fabric approximately 21 threads to 2.5 cm, 150 cm (59 in.) wide.

Milward International Range tapestry needle No. 24.

Mark the centre of fabric both ways with a line of basting stitches; on each line mark a square centrally 170 threads each way and 74 threads from crossed basting stitches. Mark the centre of each square across the fabric. The design is worked over 2 threads of fabric, approximately 10 crosses to 2.5 cm. Diagrams on pages 38-41 give the designs used on the tablecloth, excluding the border, centres indicated by blank arrows which should coincide with the basting stitches within the squares. The diagram on page 42 gives a section of the border design, centre indicated by blank arrow which should coincide with the main basting stitches. On these diagrams, each background square represents 2 threads of fabric. The layout diagram on page 43 gives one quarter of the design, showing the position of the border, with the broken lines indicating the main basting stitches and the dotted lines indicating the squares. The numbers on this diagram represent the threads of the fabric. Commence the embroidery centrally in each square and follow diagrams and sign keys for the designs. For the border, commence at the blank arrow on the diagram on page 42, 104 threads from lower edge of square and work section given. Complete one quarter following the layout diagram on page 43. Work other three quarters to correspond. Press the embroidery on the wrong side. Trim margins even. Make up, taking 2.5 cm hems.

ENGLAND

SCOTLAND

IRELAND

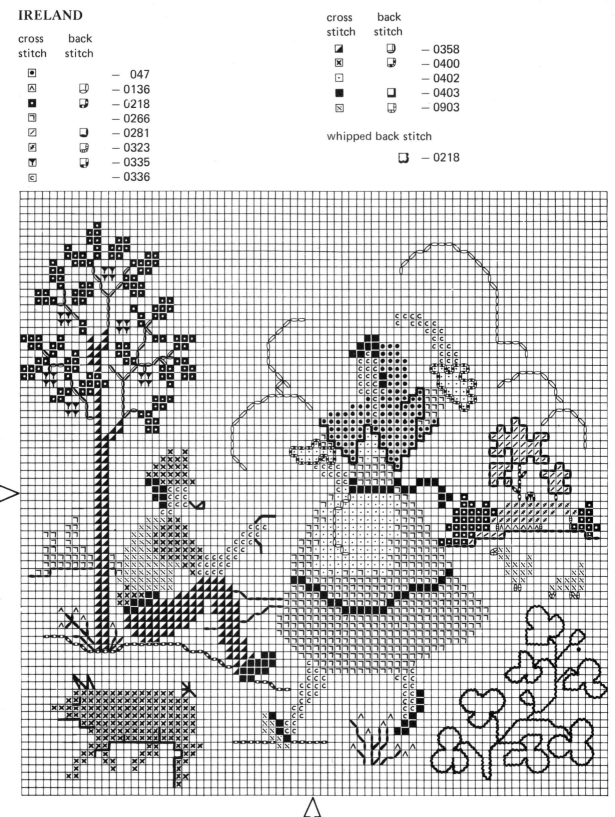

WALES

cross stitch	back stitch	
⊙		— 022
⊘		— 046
⊞		— 062
Λ	▣	— 0136
⊠		— 0139
⊚	▫	— 0263
⊓	▣	— 0266

cross stitch	back stitch	
☑		— 0295
⊠	▫	— 0314
⊆		— 0336
◪	▫	— 0358
	▣	— 0400
⊡	▫	— 0402
■	▫	— 0403
⊠		— 0903

41

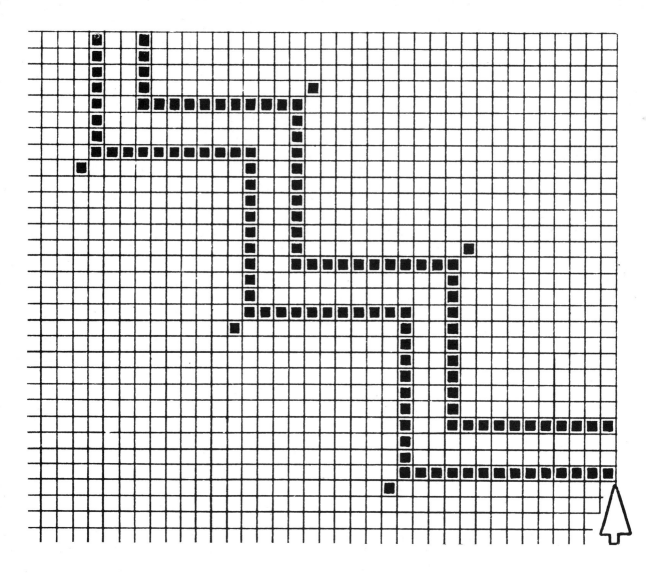

cross stitch

◼ – 0403

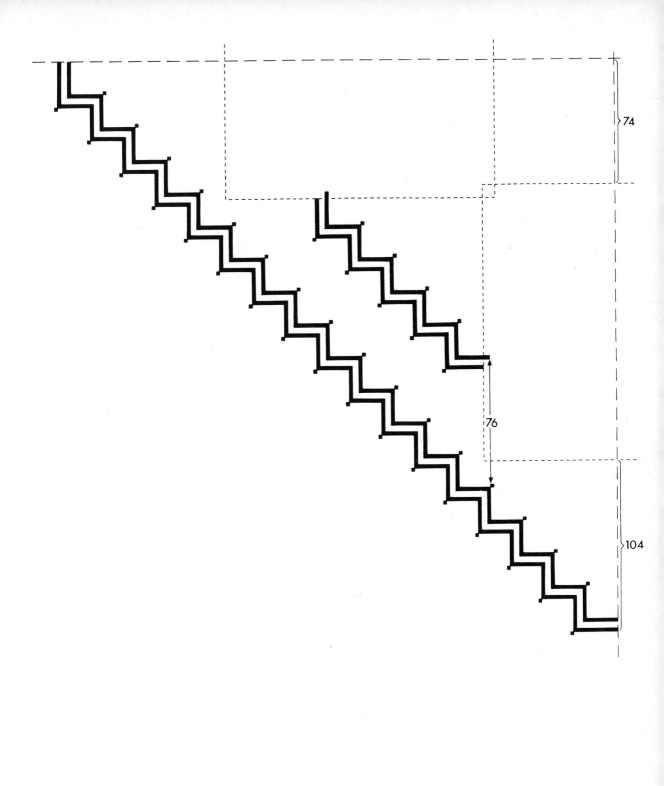

74

76

104

Cushion cover – free style – Great Britain

'Art Nouveau' has returned to the scene and is popular in all forms of design and this cushion shows a certain influence.

Materials

Clark's Anchor Stranded Cotton: 5 skeins Jade 0188; 4 skeins each Forest Green 0212, Tangerine 0311; 3 skeins Tangerine 0316. Use 12 strands for double knot stitch, 6 strands for buttonhole stitch and stem stitch, 4 strands for remainder of embroidery.
90 cm green, medium weight furnishing fabric, 122 cm (48 in.) wide.
Pad to fit.
1.30 m piping cord, size No. 4.
Milward International Range chenille needle No. 18 for 12 strands and crewel needles Nos. 5 and 6 for 6 and 4 strands respectively.

Cut a piece from fabric 43 cm square, fold across the centre both ways and crease lightly. The drawing on page 45 gives a little more than an eighth of the design, broken lines indicate the centre which should coincide with the folds. Trace the eighth as given and, omitting inner section, repeat seven times more, moving in a clockwise direction. To complete the design, trace inner section to correspond. Follow the diagram on page 46 and number key for the embroidery. All parts similar to numbered parts are worked in the same colour and stitch. Press the embroidery on the wrong side. Make a paper pattern of a circle, 43 cm in diameter. Place pattern centrally over embroidered piece of fabric and cut out. From remaining fabric, cut a circle the same size for backing and a strip 7.5 cm wide by required length for gusset. Join as necessary. Cut number of bias strips required for covering the piping cord. 1.5 cm has been allowed for seams. To make up, fold bias strip in half lengthwise wrong sides together. Insert the piping cord. Baste and stitch close to the cord. Place piping to the right side of embroidered piece, raw edges even and joining the ends to fit, baste. Baste gusset in position on embroidered piece, right sides together, raw edges even and joining ends to fit. Stitch close to the piping cord. Baste and stitch backing fabric to the remaining side of gusset, right sides together, leaving an opening for pad insertion. Turn to right side. Insert pad and slipstitch open edges together.

45

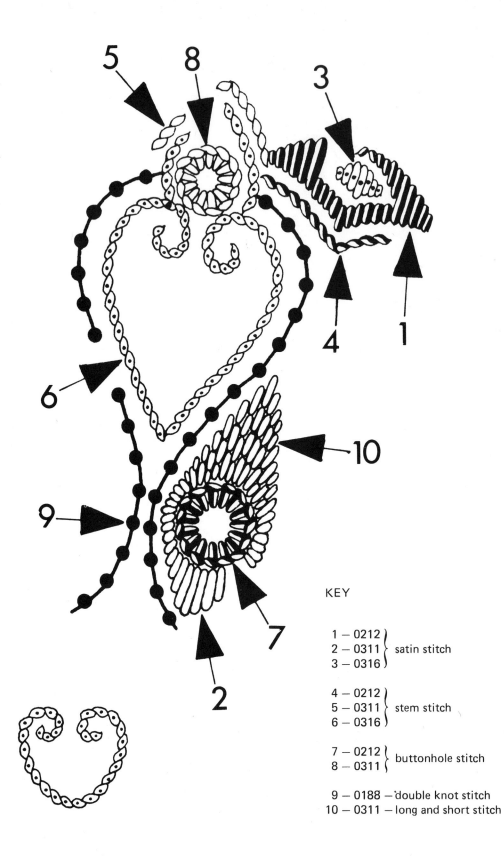

KEY

1 — 0212 ⎫
2 — 0311 ⎬ satin stitch
3 — 0316 ⎭

4 — 0212 ⎫
5 — 0311 ⎬ stem stitch
6 — 0316 ⎭

7 — 0212 ⎫
8 — 0311 ⎬ buttonhole stitch

9 — 0188 — double knot stitch
10 — 0311 — long and short stitch

Lunch mats—cut work—Italy

Italy, along with France, was one of the main pioneers of cut-work. This style of embroidery is known by other names depending upon the intricacy of the design and use of stitchery. This model, though not quite so delicate as earlier examples, still retains the essential characteristics of the technique, but it is more practical for everyday use than its lace-like predecessors.

Materials

Clark's Anchor Pearl Cotton No. 8 (10g ball): 1 ball each Parrot Green 0255, Moss Green 0267, Gorse Yellow 0304.

50 cm white medium weight embroidery fabric, 137 cm (54 in.) wide.

Milward International Range crewel needle No. 6.

Cut two pieces from fabric, 45 x 50 cm and fold
across the centre of each both ways and crease lightly.
The drawing on page 49 gives a section of the design,
broken line indicates the centre, which should coincide
with the widthwise fold. Dotted lines indicate the position of the repeat. Parts marked X on the drawing and
black on the diagram are the sections of fabric to be
cut away after the embroidery is completed. With one
long side of fabric facing, trace section as given 9.5 cm
from centre. To complete one long side, repeat in
reverse from broken line. Turn fabric and trace other
long side in the same way. With one short side of
fabric facing and omitting corner motif, trace section
in position indicated. Trace other short side in the
same way. Follow the diagram and number key for
the embroidery. All parts similar to numbered parts
are worked in the same colour and stitch. It is important to have the looped edge of the buttonhole stitch
to the sections of fabric to be cut away. Press the
embroidery on the wrong side. Using small sharp
pointed scissors and cutting from the wrong side, cut
away the surplus fabric around the edge and all parts
marked X on the drawing.

KEY

1 — 0255) ⎱
2 — 0267) ⎰ buttonhole stitch
3 — 0304)
4 — 0255 — stem stitch
5 — 0304 — satin stitch
6 — 0267 — straight stitch
7 — 0267 — fly stitch

49

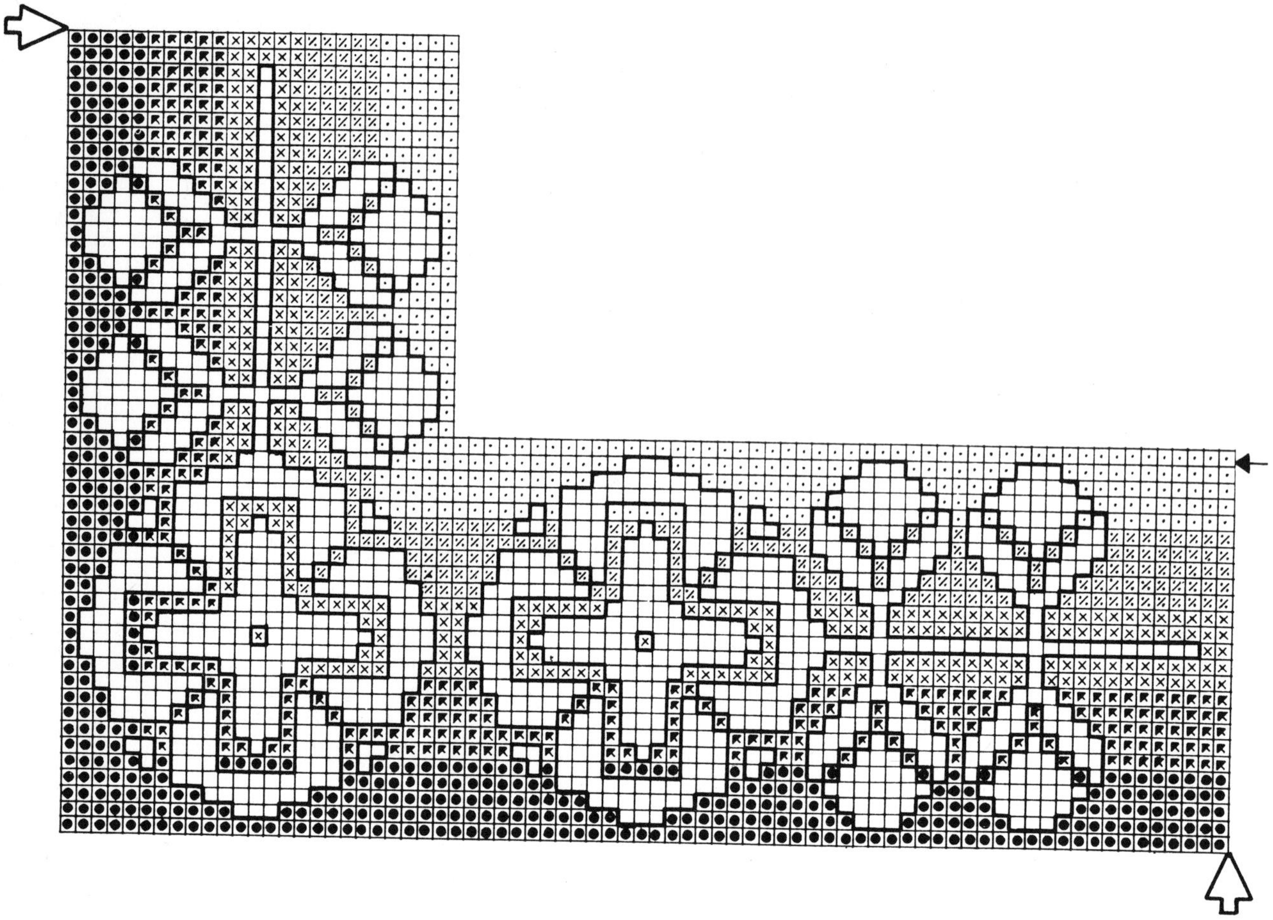

KEY

▨	—	0357
☒	—	0358
⊡	—	0368
▧	—	0369
◉	—	0382

cross stitch

◻	—	0382 — Holbein stitch

Lunch mats–Assisi–Italy

Italy has a fabulous background of traditional embroidery of many styles and techniques, but much of it was very delicate and more suited to the care of a museum than for use in the modern home. However, one Italian legacy which we have inherited is the famous Assisi embroidery. It is very simple to work, using only cross stitch and Holbein stitch, the latter being double running stitch. The design on the lunch mats is a modern interpretation of Assisi embroidery, not the traditional style with the background of cross stitch surrounding the motifs embroidered in blue or terra cotta, outlined with black, but a subtle shading of brown and tan.

Materials

Clark's Anchor Stranded Cotton: 15 skeins Coffee 0382; 5 skeins each Oak Brown 0357, Peat Brown 0358; 4 skeins each Cinnamon 0368, 0369. Use 4 strands throughout.
40 cm beige evenweave embroidery fabric, 21 threads to 2.5 cm, 150 cm (59 in.) wide.
Milward International Range tapestry needle No. 24.

Cut three pieces from fabric 36 x 50 cm and mark the centre of each piece both ways with a line of basting stitches. The diagram on page 50 gives a quarter of the design, centre indicated by blank arrows, which should coincide with the basting stitches. The design is worked in cross stitch and Holbein stitch over 2 threads of fabric and it is important that the upper half of all crosses lie in the same direction. When using cross stitch combined with Holbein stitch all the cross stitches are worked first. It is then easier to keep the Holbein stitch straight and regular. Each background square on the diagram represents 2 threads of fabric. Commence the design at small black arrow, 52 threads down from crossed basting stitches and work the section given. Work other three quarters to correspond. Press the embroidery on the wrong side. To make up, turn back 1.5 cm hems, mitre corners and slipstitch.

Wall hanging–Rya stitch–Finland

This wall hanging includes Rya stitch, a development of the technique used in the making of the famous Rya rugs. These rugs in their original form may be found in most of the Scandinavian countries. Finland was one of the pioneers of this craft, and here is a unique embroidered version. This stitch produces a fascinating three dimensional texture with a play of light and shade on the yarn.

Materials

Coats Anchor Tapisserie Wool: 7 skeins Amber Gold 0306; 3 skeins Gold 0500; 2 skeins each Muscat Green 0279, Buttercup 0297, Amber Gold 0305, Sage Green 0842; 1 skein Amber Gold 0563.
50 cm dark brown, square weave fabric, 107 cm (42 in.) wide, approximately 6 holes to 2.5 cm.
50 cm matching lining fabric, 91 (36 in.) wide.
Coats Drima (polyester) multi-purpose thread.
Rod 1.5 cm in diameter, 51 cm in length.
Milward International Range tapestry needle No. 18.

Cut a piece from fabric 46 x 58.5 cm and mark the centre both ways with a line of basting stitches. The diagram on page 54 gives half of the design, blank arrows indicate the centre which should coincide with the basting stitches. Each background square on the diagram represents one square of fabric. The design is worked in cross stitch (each stitch over one square of fabric, with the upper half of all crosses lying in the same direction) and Rya stitch (each stitch worked horizontally along a line of holes represented on the diagram with ellipses). Following the diagram and number key for the embroidery, commence the design centrally and work the given half working the cross stitch area first, then the rows of Rya stitch commencing from the bottom row upwards, the fringe approximately 6.5 cm deep with each row overlapping the preceding row by 1.5 cm. Work right half to correspond. Press embroidery on the wrong side. To make up, cut out hanging to shape as shown in photograph or as desired, allowing 1.5 cm seams all round except at top edge where 5 cm of fabric is required for centre tabs and 10 cm for side tabs. Cut a piece from lining the same size as fabric. Place lining to embroidered piece right sides together. Baste and stitch close to embroidery, leaving an opening to turn to right side. Trim fabric, clip corners and turn to right side. Slipstitch open edges together. Fold over top tabs to wrong side to form loops and sew in position. Insert rod.

Rya stitch, page 55.

This stitch is worked from left to right, and from the bottom row upwards, using four thicknesses of thread; for simplicity the stitch diagram shows one thickness only. Figure 1. Bring the thread through at the arrow, insert the needle two holes to the right at A, bring through one hole to the left at B keeping the thread above the needle. Figure 2. Insert the needle at C one hole to the right of A and bring through at A one hole to the left, keeping the thread below the needle. Hold down the loop of thread, the required length with left thumb and continue in this way to end of row. Figure 3. When complete cut the loops of thread to form fringe.

enlarged detail opposite

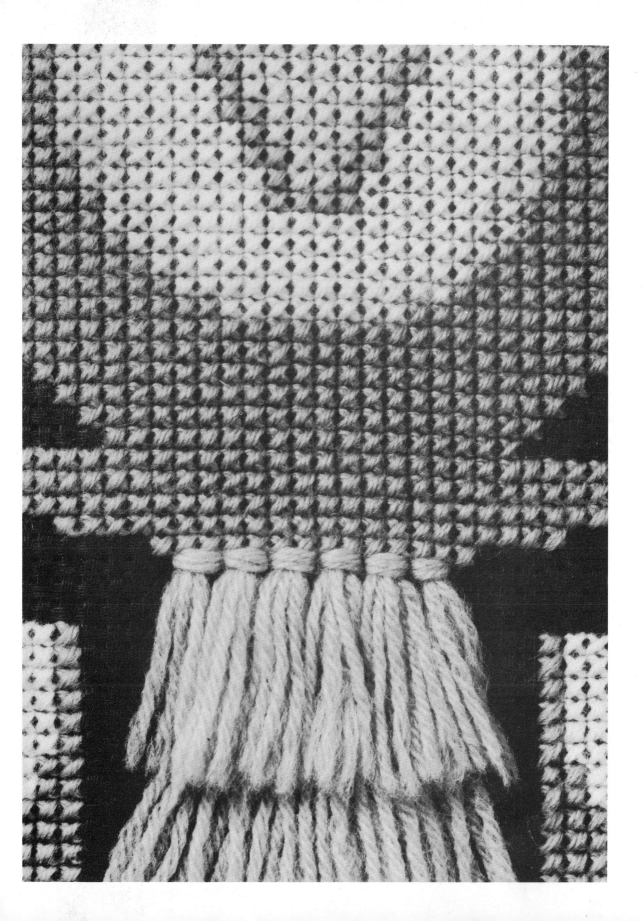

1 — 0297 ⎫
2 — 0305 ⎬
3 — 0306 ⎭ cross stitch

4 — 0500 ⎫
5 — 0563 ⎬
6 — 0842 ⎭

A — 0279 ⎫
B — 0306 ⎬ Rya stitch
C — 0500 ⎭

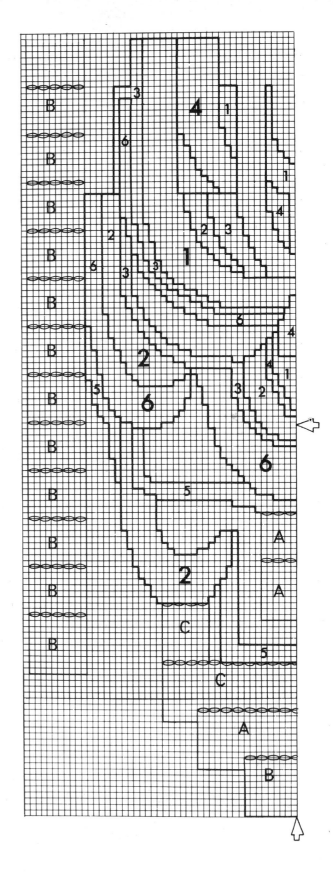

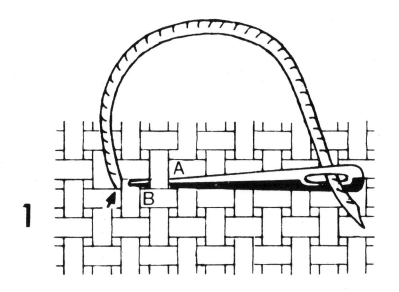

1

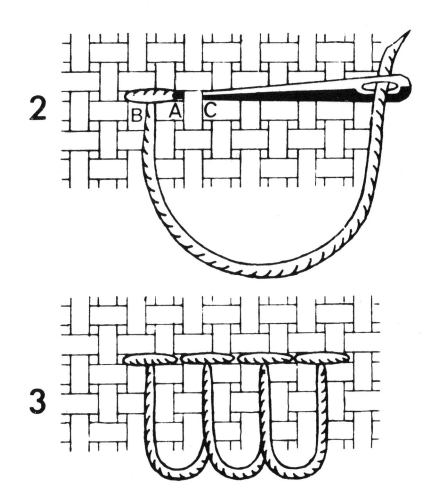

2

3

Traycloth—free style—Spain

The designers of these two models have broken away from their traditional design and stitch techniques and produced delicate interpretations of flowers, leaves and berries.

Materials

Clark's Anchor Stranded Cotton: 2 skeins Electric Blue 0142; 1 skein each Petunia 092, Violet 0101, Electric Blue 0140. Use 3 strands for stem stitch, 4 strands for remainder of embroidery.

40 cm grey medium weight embroidery fabric, 91 cm (36 in.) wide.

1 each Milward International Range crewel needles Nos. 7 and 6 for 3 and 4 strands respectively.

Cut a piece from fabric 38 x 52 cm and fold in half lengthwise and crease lightly. The drawing gives a section of the design, centre marked by broken line, which should coincide with the fold. With one short side facing trace section as given 3 cm from lower edge. Leaving no space between repeat section, excluding area within dotted outline, twice more to the right to complete one short side. Turn fabric and trace other short side in same way. Follow the diagram on page 57 and the number key for the embroidery. All parts similar to numbered parts are worked in the same colour and stitch. Press the embroidery on the wrong side. Turn back 1.5 cm hems, mitre corners and stitch.

KEY

1 — 092) ⎫
2 — 0140) ⎬ chain stitch
3 — 0101 — stem stitch
4 — 0142 — stem stitch filling

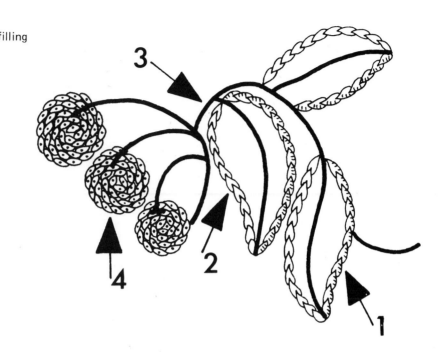

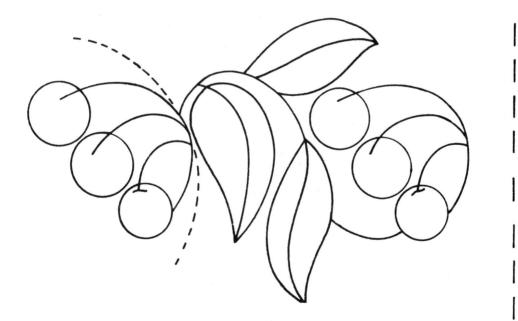

Powder compact cover –free style–Spain

Materials

Clark's Anchor Stranded Cotton: 1 skein each Buttercup 0292, Amber Gold 0308, Tangerine 0313, Terra Cotta 0341. Use 3 strands for embroidery and 1 strand in matching colour for beads.

20 cm medium weight turquoise dress fabric 91 cm (36 in.) wide.

1 piece iron-on Vilene or other iron-on interlining 23 x 13 x cm.

24 turquoise beads.

40 cm matching cord.

1 each Milward International Range crewel needle No. 7 and beading needle.

Coats Drima (polyester) multi-purpose thread.

Cut 1 piece from fabric 15 x 15 cm. Fold in half both ways and crease lightly. The drawing gives the complete design, centre indicated by broken lines which should coincide with the folds. Trace the design centrally. Follow the diagram on this page and number key for the embroidery. All parts similar to numbered parts are worked in the same colour, stitch and bead. Press the embroidery on the wrong side before sewing on the beads. To make up. 1.5 cm has been allowed for seams. Trim embroidered section to 12.5 cm square keeping embroidery central. Cut a piece from fabric 12.5 cm square for back section. Cut a piece of fabric 23 x 13 cm for lining. Baste and sew embroidered front section to back section, right sides together, leaving top edge open. Trim seams and turn to right side. Iron interlining to wrong side of lining section. Fold lining section in half lengthwise, right sides together. Baste and sew side seams. Trim seams. Insert lining in cover. Turn in and baste seam allowance on top edge of lining and embroidered section. Sew round top edge and attach cord.

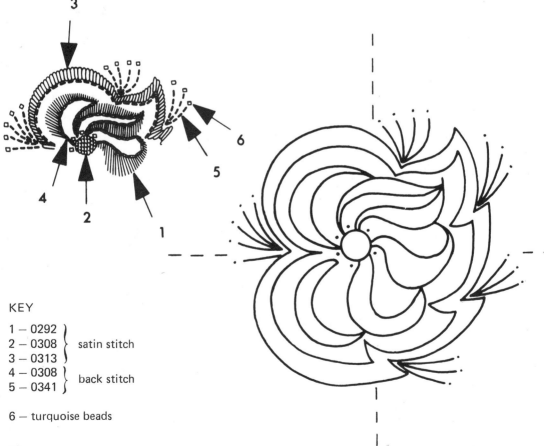

KEY

1 – 0292 ⎫
2 – 0308 ⎬ satin stitch
3 – 0313 ⎭

4 – 0308 ⎫
5 – 0341 ⎬ back stitch

6 – turquoise beads

Owl panel – free style – Norway

Norway has a long history of traditional embroidery — two world famous styles are Hardanger and Akle. Today, Norwegian designers, though not forgetting the past, are entering the field of modern design and this delightful Owl panel is a superb example.

Materials

Clark's Anchor Stranded Cotton: 2 skeins Peat Brown 0358; 1 skein each Gorse Yellow 0301, Tangerine 0313, Orange 0323, 0326, Cream 0386, White 0402, Black 0403. Use 2 strands for back stitch, fly stitch and straight stitch, 3 strands for rest of embroidery.

50 cm royal blue medium weight embroidery fabric 91 cm (36 in.)wide.

Picture frame with mounting board or cardboard 42 x 32 cm.

1 each Milward International Range crewel needles No. 8 for 2 strands, No. 7 for 3 strands.

Mounting and framing instructions see page 11.

Cut a piece from fabric 50 x 51 cm. The drawing on page 62 gives the complete design. Trace as given centrally on to fabric. Follow the diagram on the facing page, and number key for the embroidery. All parts similar to numbered parts are worked in the same colour and stitch. To complete the design work four straight stitches in Tangerine within each curve made by cable chain stitch. Press the embroidery on the wrong side.

KEY

1 — 0301	
2 — 0313	
3 — 0323	back stitch
4 — 0358	
5 — 0403	
6 — 0386	
7 — 0402	satin stitch
8 — 0403	
9 — 0326	
10 — 0402	straight stitch
11 — 0301	
12 — 0326	buttonhole stitch
13 — 0301	
14 — 0323	
15 — 0326	fly stitch
16 — 0402	
17 — 0326	
18 — 0358	chain stitch
19 — 0301	
20 — 0403	leaf stitch
21 — 0313	
22 — 0323	stem stitch
23 — 0313 — cable chain stitch	
24 — 0313 — double knot stitch	
25 — 0358 — whipped back stitch	

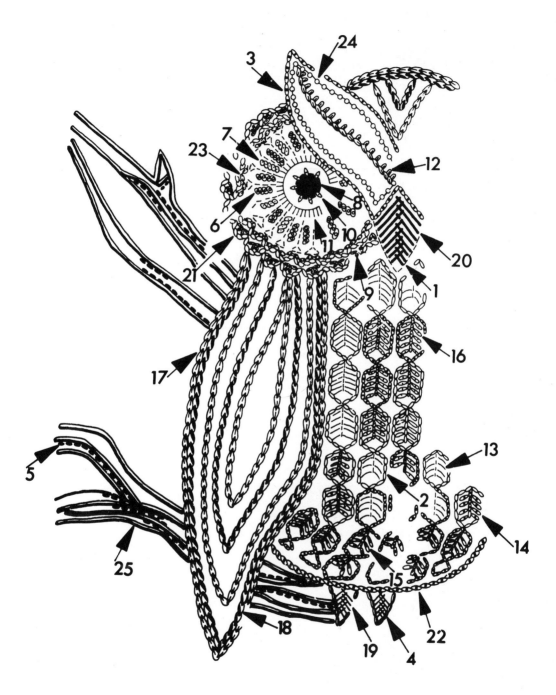

Trolley cloth – free style – Sweden

In both these pieces of embroidery one can appreciate the ability of Swedish designers to bring vibrant colour and simplicity of design to their work.

Materials
Clark's Anchor Stranded Cotton: 6 skeins Orange 0324; 2 skeins Coffee 0382; 1 skein each Rose Pink 054, Snuff Brown 0375. Use 4 strands throughout.
50 cm white furnishing fabric, 122 cm (48 in.) wide.
Milward International Range crewel needle No. 6.

Cut a piece from fabric 44.5 x 64.5 cm. Fold in half both ways and crease lightly. The drawing on page 65 gives a section of the design. With one long side of

fabric facing trace section within bracket, with the broken line coinciding with the widthwise fold 6 mm down from lengthwise fold. Trace the complete section to the left. Repeat in reverse on to right-hand side. Turn the fabric and trace other half in same way. Follow the diagram on page 65 and number key for the embroidery. All parts similar to numbered parts are worked in the same colour and stitch. Press embroidery on the wrong side. To make up, turn back 1.5 cm hems, mitre corners and stitch.

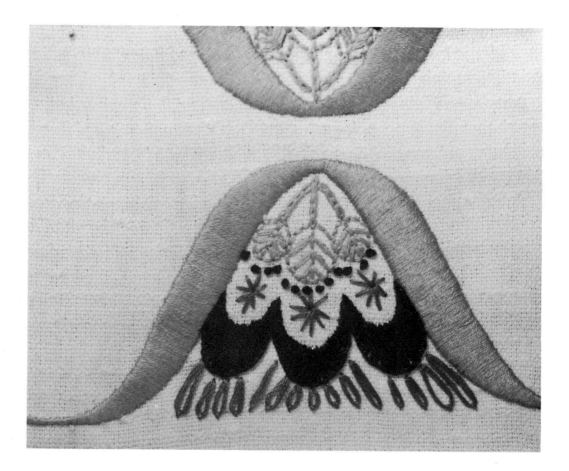

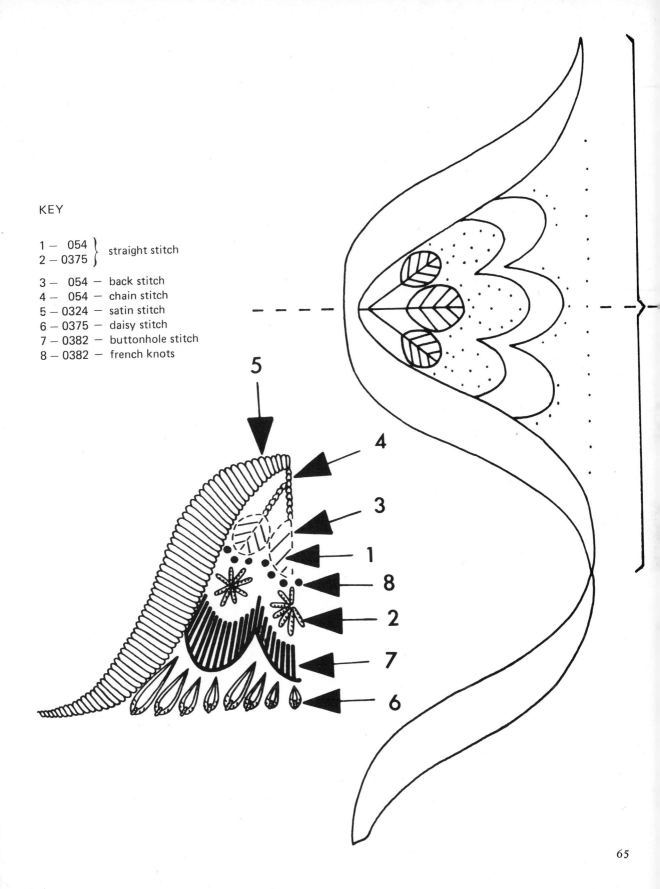

KEY

1 — 054 ⎫
2 — 0375 ⎬ straight stitch

3 — 054 — back stitch
4 — 054 — chain stitch
5 — 0324 — satin stitch
6 — 0375 — daisy stitch
7 — 0382 — buttonhole stitch
8 — 0382 — french knots

5

4

3

1

8

2

7

6

Cushion cover—free style—Sweden

Materials
Clark's Anchor Soft Embroidery: 2 skeins each Terra Cotta 0340, Beige 0379, Coffee 0381, Grey 0401; 1 skein Cinnamon 0368.
60 cm ecru medium weight furnishing fabric 122 cm (48 in.) wide.
Milward International Range chenille needle No. 18.

Cut 2 pieces from fabric 60 x 60 cm. Fold one piece in half both ways and crease lightly. The drawing on page 68 gives a quarter of the design, centre indicated by broken lines, which should coincide with the folds. Trace as given on to lower right-hand quarter. Trace other three quarters in same way. Each quarter has a different colour scheme. Follow the diagram and number keys on page 69 for the embroidery. All parts similar to numbered parts are worked in the same colour and stitch. To make up, place back and front right sides together and stitch 2.5 cm from edge, leaving an opening to allow the pad to be easily inserted. Press seams and turn to right side. Insert pad. Turn in seam allowance and slipstitch together.

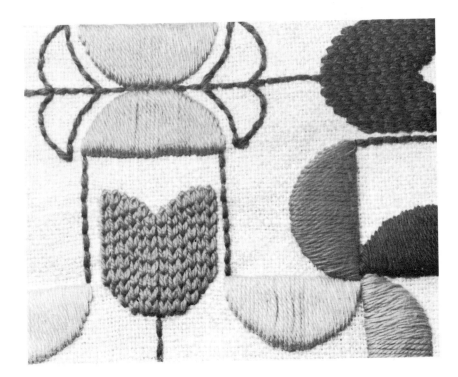

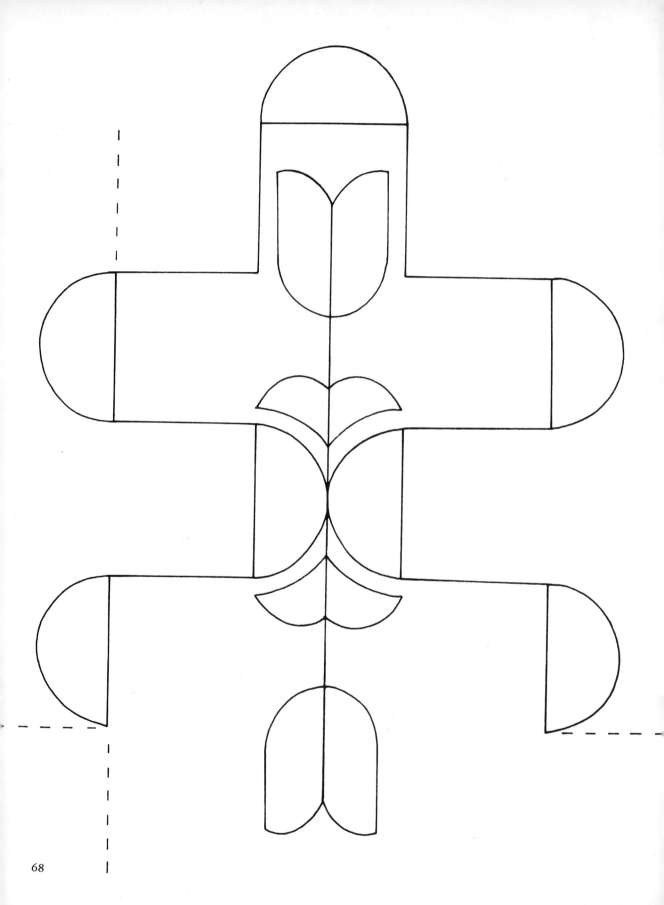

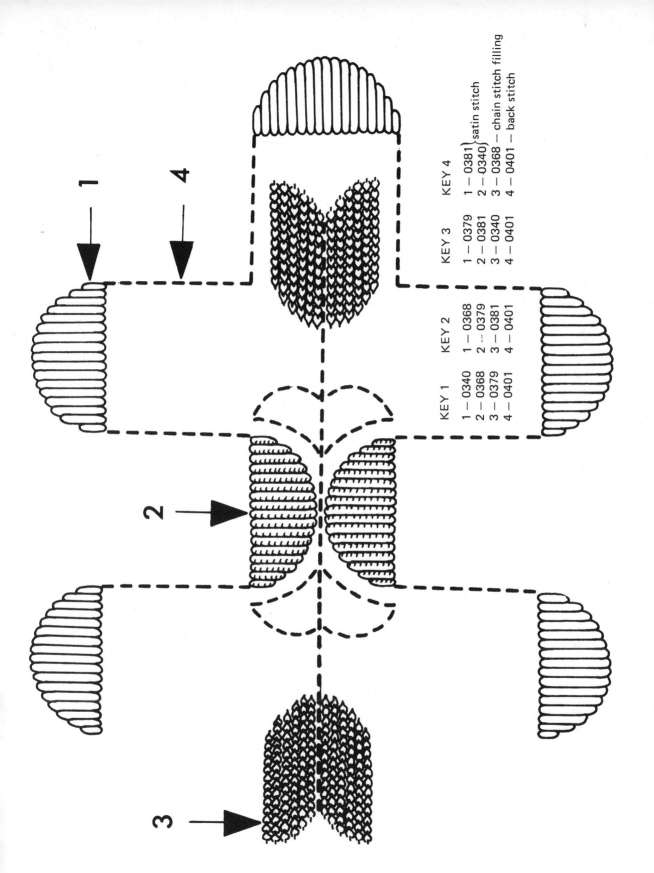

1

4

2

3

KEY 1

1 — 0340
2 — 0368
3 — 0379
4 — 0401

KEY 2

1 — 0368
2 — 0379
3 — 0381
4 — 0401

KEY 3

1 — 0379
2 — 0381
3 — 0340
4 — 0401

KEY 4

1 — 0381
2 — 0340 } satin stitch
3 — 0368 — chain stitch filling
4 — 0401 — back stitch

69

Lampshade–shadow work–France

Shadow work is one of the most delicate and beautiful types of embroidery. Its main feature is the use of transparent fabric and the 'shadow' effect achieved by the embroidery, which is worked on the reverse side of the fabric. This style of embroidery is thought to be of Indian origin. These two designs illustrate how French embroiderers have interpreted this technique.

Materials

Clark's Anchor Stranded Cotton: 3 skeins Chestnut 0352. Use 2 strands throughout.

50 cm lemon organdie or other similar transparent fabric, 115 cm (45 in.) wide.

Piece 90.8 x 31.8 cm white bonding parchment, or non-adhesive lampshade parchment.

2 lampshade rings 28 cm in diameter, one with fitting.

Coats Nainsook bias binding, white, for binding rings.

1 tube fabric adhesive.

1 m. 90 cm gimp for edging (to be used with non-adhesive lampshade parchment).

Coats Drima (polyester) multi-purpose thread.

1 Milward International Range crewel needle No. 8.

The drawing on page 73 gives the complete large motif, with the section used for small motif indicated by broken lines. With one long side of fabric facing, trace the large motif as given, 7.5 cm from right-hand selvedge and 8.8 cm from lower edge, then trace the small motif 3.2 cm to left of large motif and 8.8 cm from lower edge. Alternating large and small motifs, trace each motif twice more, spacing evenly. Follow the diagram on page 74 and number key for embroidery. All parts similar to numbered parts are worked in the same stitch. Press embroidery on wrong side.

To make up. Place bonding parchment on flat surface, shiny side up. With one long side of parchment facing, place fabric on top, wrong side towards parchment, with large motif 3.8 cm from right-hand side and all motifs 3.2 cm from lower edge, leaving surplus fabric to overlap edges. Hold in position with paper clips or weights, and iron fabric on to parchment. Trim fabric, leaving 1.3 cm on long sides and left-hand short side; trim fabric level with parchment on right-hand short side. Spread adhesive on left margin and stick to inside of parchment. Bind rings tightly, overlapping edges of binding. Pin the fabric-covered parchment in position around the rings. Fold seam allowance in half and using small stitches, sew to top ring starting at raw short side and stopping about 5 cm from other side. Stitch the lower ring in position in the same way. Overlap finished short side and stick in position. Finish sewing at upper and lower edges. If non-adhesive parchment is used for backing, overlap short ends of parchment to fit rings and glue together. Sew rings to top and lower edges. Baste and stitch short ends of fabric, right sides together to fit over frame. Trim seam if necessary. Turn to right side, pull fabric over frame and sew to rings. To finish off this method attach gimp by sticking to upper and lower edges to cover stitching.

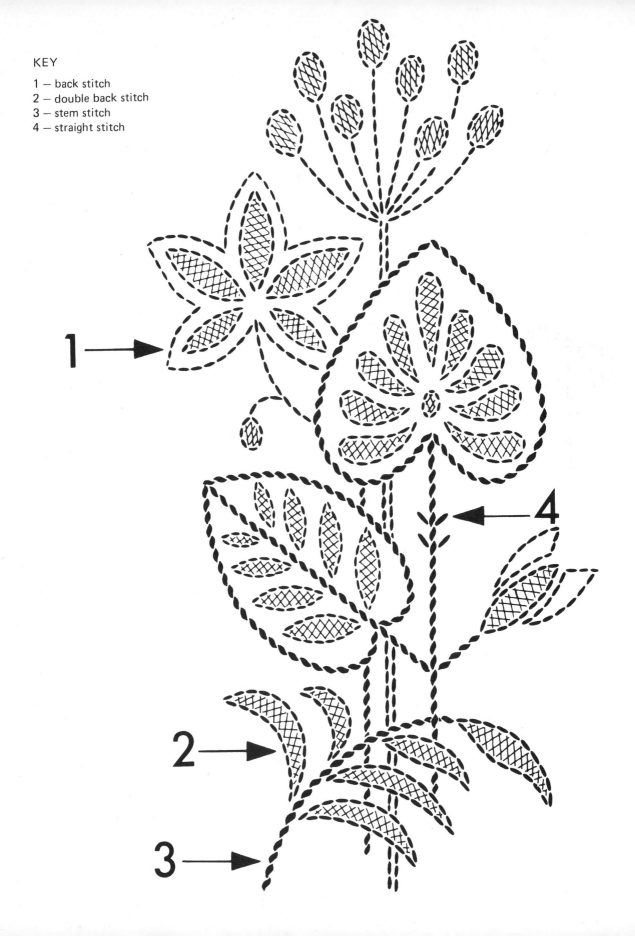

KEY

1 — back stitch
2 — double back stitch
3 — stem stitch
4 — straight stitch

1

4

2

3

Cheval set—shadow work—France

Materials
Clark's Anchor Stranded Cotton: 3 skeins White 0402;
2 skeins Cobalt Blue 0132. Use 2 strands throughout.
60 cm blue fine transparent fabric, 115 cm (45 in.)
wide.
1 Milward International Range crewel needle No. 8.

Cut one piece from fabric 65 cm x 39.5 cm and two
pieces 24 cm square. Fold each piece across the
centre both ways and crease lightly. The drawing on
page 76 gives one quarter of the design as used on
the runner, centre marked by broken lines which
should coincide with the folds; the section within the
dotted line indicates one quarter of the design as used
on the small mats. With one long side of runner facing,
trace as given on to lower left-hand quarter. Repeat in
reverse on to lower right-hand quarter omitting flower
shape on vertical fold. Turn fabric and repeat on other
two quarters. Trace section within dotted line on to
small mats in same way. Follow the diagram on page
78 and number key for the embroidery. All parts
similar to numbered parts are worked in the same
colour and stitch. Press the embroidery on the wrong
side. Turn back 1.5 cm hem on all sides, mitre corners
and stitch.

enlarged detail

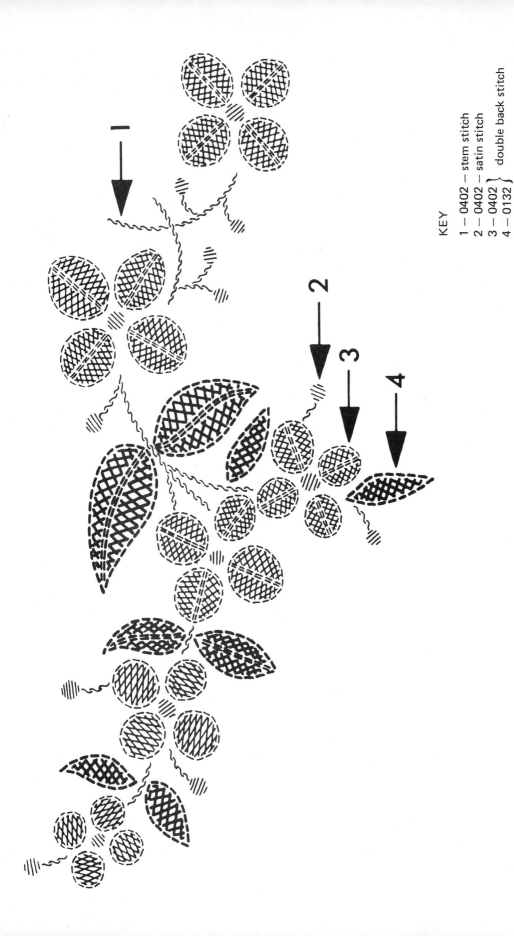

KEY

1 — 0402 — stem stitch
2 — 0402 — satin stitch
3 — 0402 }
4 — 0132 } double back stitch

Lunch mats—counted thread—Sweden

There is no doubt that over thirty years ago Sweden was the forerunner of modern embroidery design. Unfortunately, it was some time before this style was generally accepted in other parts of Europe, many still controlled by their own traditions. Today, the simplicity of design and the use of sparkling colour have made embroidery designs from Sweden readily acceptable throughout the world. One must admire the skill of their designers, who retain a certain amount of realism, combined with superb form and colour.

Materials
Coats Anchor Tapisserie Wool: 2 skeins Spring Green 0238; 1 skein each Emerald 0229, Moss Green 0265, Muscat Green 0281.
40 cm cream medium weight evenweave fabric, 18 threads to 2.5 cm, 142 cm (56 in.) wide.
Milward International Range tapestry needle No. 18.

Cut two pieces from fabric, 40 x 50 cm, and mark the centre of each piece both ways with a line of basting stitches. The diagram gives a section of the design and on page 81 shows the arrangement of the stitches on the threads of the fabric, represented by the background lines. With one long side of fabric facing, commence the design at small black arrow, 42 threads down and 100 threads to the left of crossed basting stitches and work the section as given, following the diagram on page 81 and number key for the embroidery. All parts similar to numbered parts are worked in the same colour and stitch. Continue working running stitch 0238 to widthwise basting stitches. To complete lower half repeat in reverse from widthwise basting stitches. Work a border of wave stitch using 0238, 11 fabric threads from running stitches and continue to lengthwise basting stitches. To complete, repeat border only on other half. Press the embroidery on the wrong side. Make a fringe, 2.5 cm in depth on all sides by withdrawing the required number of threads.

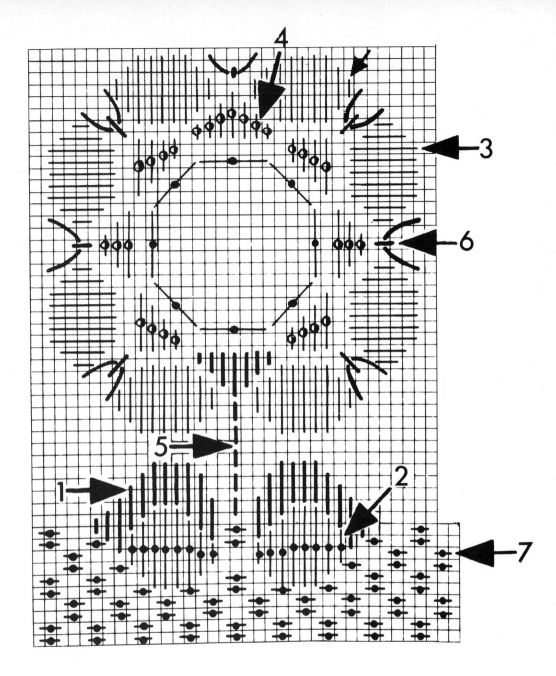

KEY

$\left.\begin{array}{l} 1 - 0229 \\ 2 - 0238 \\ 3 - 0265 \\ 4 - 0281 \end{array}\right\}$ satin stitch

5 — 0229 — back stitch
6 — 0229 — fly stitch
7 — 0238 — running stitch

Tablecloth–cross stitch–Denmark

For many years Danish designers have held an eminent position in the world of cross stitch design — exquisite pictures in very fine stitchery which are so realistic they might have been painted. This tablecloth is bolder and more stylised, but still retains natural forms in its design.

Materials

Clark's Anchor Stranded Cotton: 6 skeins Muscat Green 0279; 4 skeins each Jade 0188, Muscat Green 0281; 3 skeins each Jade 0186, Orange 0326. Use 4 strands throughout.

1.50 m beige evenweave embroidery fabric 21 threads to 2.5 cm, 150 cm (59 in.) wide.

Milward International Range tapestry needle No. 24.

Mark the centre both ways with a line of basting stitches. The diagram on page 84, gives A and B and corner turning C. The centre is marked by blank arrow which should coincide with the basting stitches. The design is worked throughout in cross stitch over 2 threads of fabric and it is important that the upper half of all crosses lie in the same direction. Each background square on the diagram represents 2 threads of fabric. Commence the design at small black arrow 119 threads down from and 29 threads to the right of crossed basting stitches and work section A and B as given repeating inner border once more to the left. Repeat section A and B then work corner turning C. To complete one quarter of the design continue in sequence to basting stitches. Work other three quarters in same way. Press the embroidery on the wrong side. To make up, turn back 2.5 cm hems, mitre corners and slipstitch.

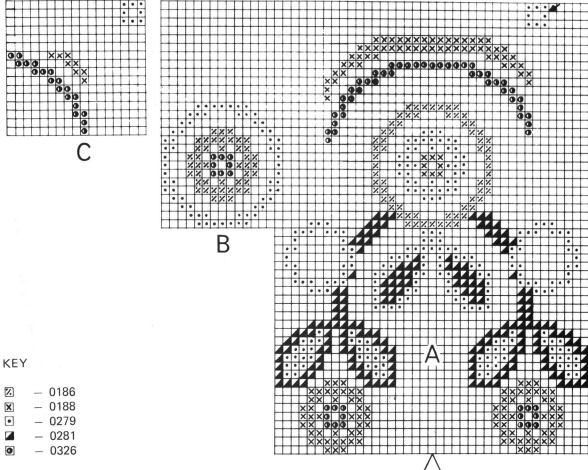

KEY

⧄	—	0186
⊠	—	0188
⊡	—	0279
◣	—	0281
⊙	—	0326

A

B

C

Runner–cross stitch–Greece and Italy

Today, foreign travel is enjoyed by many people and Greece and Italy are favourite spots. Both Greece and Italy have long traditions of embroidery, but this table runner incorporates local scenes rather than techniques — in fact, all worked in simple cross stitch. This runner could be a reminder of one of your holidays.

Materials

Clark's Anchor Stranded Cotton: 2 skeins Peat Brown 0358, 1 skein each Cardinal 019, Carnation 025, 029, Raspberry 069, Parma Violet 0110, 0112, Electric Blue 0142, Peacock Blue 0170, Laurel Green 0208, Forest Green 0218, Almond Green 0261, Moss Green 0265, Amber Gold 0305, Terra Cotta 0336, Chestnut 0349, Snuff Brown 0375, Grey 0400, White 0402 and Black 0403. Use 3 strands throughout.

Quantities if required individually — 1 skein of each colour quoted on the appropriate diagram for each country and 2 skeins for the border.

50 cm white or natural medium weight evenweave fabric, approximately 21 threads to 2.5 cm, 150 cm (59 in.) wide.

Milward International Range tapestry needle No. 24.

Cut one piece from fabric 46 x 113 cm. Mark the centre both ways with a line of basting stitches. The design is worked over 2 threads of fabric, approximately 10 crosses to 2.5 cm. The diagrams on pages 88 and 89 give the designs used on the runner, excluding the border, centres indicated by blank arrows. The diagram on page 87 gives a section of the border design (A) centre indicated by blank arrow which should coincide with the widthwise basting stitches and also gives a corner turning (B). Each background square on the diagrams represents 2 threads of fabric. With one long side of fabric facing, commence the embroidery with the border at blank arrow on section A, 138 threads down from crossed basting stitches and work section given, following the diagram and sign key. Repeat section 18 times to the left then

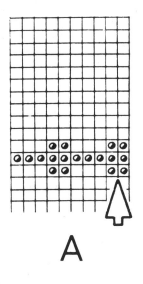

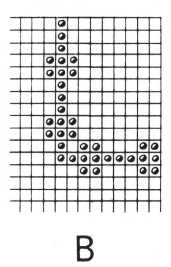

KEY

⊘ — 0358 — cross stitch

A

B

work section B. Continue along short side to basting stitches to complete one quarter of the border. Work other three quarters to correspond. Mark a 20.3 cm square with basting stitches centrally 2.5 cm from border at each short end. Mark the centre of each square widthwise on the fabric.   With short end facing, commence the design centrally within the square and follow the diagrams and appropriate sign key for each end. Press the embroidery on the wrong side. Trim fabric to within 5 cm from border on short sides and 4 cm on long sides. Make up, taking 1.5 cm hems.

GREECE

cross stitch	back stitch	
⬚		— 019
⊠		— 069
⊙	⊐	— 0170
▪	⊐	— 0218
⬚	⊐	— 0265
⬚		— 0305

cross stitch	back stitch	
C		— 0336
⬚		— 0349
◣		— 0358
⬚	⊐	— 0375
	⊐	— 0400
⬚		— 0402
■	⊐	— 0403

88

cross stitch	back stitch	
�face		— 025
✖		— 029
∧		— 0110
Y		— 0112
⊙	⊔	— 0142
⁄		— 0208
■	⊔	— 0218

cross stitch	back stitch	
⊞	⊔	— 0261
⊘	⊔	— 0305
C		— 0336
◢	⊔	— 0358
◨	⊔	— 0375
✗	⊔	— 0400
·		— 0402
■	⊔	— 0403

Trolley cloth – free style – Switzerland

Switzerland has long been famed for its embroidery, often termed as Swiss Lace, owing to its delicacy. Now this style of embroidery is being made by the metre, with the help of the most sophisticated embroidery machines in St. Gall. Here is a modern example of embroidery from Switzerland done by hand.

Materials
Clark's Anchor Stranded Cotton: 2 skeins each Muscat Green 0280, Gorse Yellow 0304; 1 skein each Buttercup 0297, Flame 0332, Terra Cotta 0341. Use 3 strands throughout.
50 cm beige embroidery fabric 91 cm (36 in.) wide.
Milward International Range crewel needle No. 7.

Cut a piece from fabric 42 x 62 cm and fold in half both ways and crease lightly. The drawing on page 93 gives a section of the design, centre marked by broken line, which should coincide with the widthwise fold; the broken outline indicates the position of the repeat. With one long side of fabric facing, trace as given on to right-hand side 15 cm down from centre fold. Repeat apple section in position indicated and repeat once more omitting green apple core. Trace small leaves as shown or as desired. Turn fabric and trace other long side in same way. Follow the diagram and number key on page 92 for embroidery. Press the embroidery on the wrong side. Turn back 1.5 cm hems, mitre corners and stitch.

enlarged detail

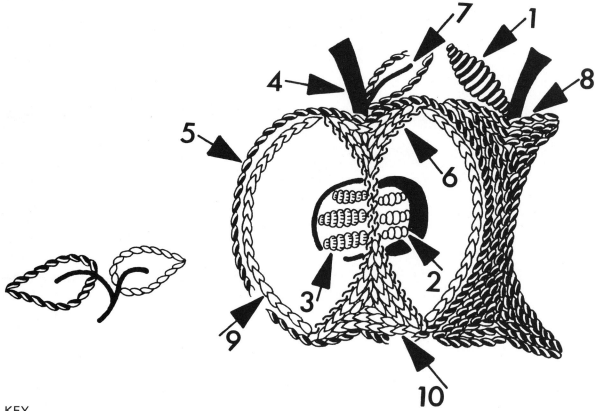

KEY

1 — 0280 ⎫
2 — 0304 ⎬ satin stitch
3 — 0332 ⎪
4 — 0341 ⎭

5 — 0280 ⎫
6 — 0297 ⎬ stem stitch
7 — 0341 ⎭

8 — 0280 — stem stitch filling
9 — 0304 — chain stitch
10 — 0304 — chain stitch filling

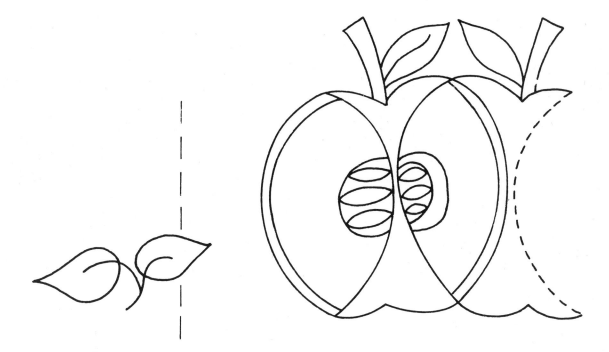

Trolley cloth – Blackwork – Spain

Blackwork embroidery is one of the most popular of the counted thread embroidery techniques. It is traditionally of Spanish origin and the designs were based on the floral forms found in the architecture and decoration of medieval Spain, which were in effect a copy in miniature of Spanish Moresque motifs. This example uses the same stitch patterns, but the designer has been influenced by the more geometric styles of today.

Materials
Clark's Anchor Stranded Cotton: 5 skeins Carmine Rose 045. Use 2 strands for whipping back stitch, 3 strands for rest of embroidery.
50 cm beige evenweave fabric, 21 threads to 2.5 cm, 150 cm (59 in.) wide.
Milward International Range tapestry needle No. 24.

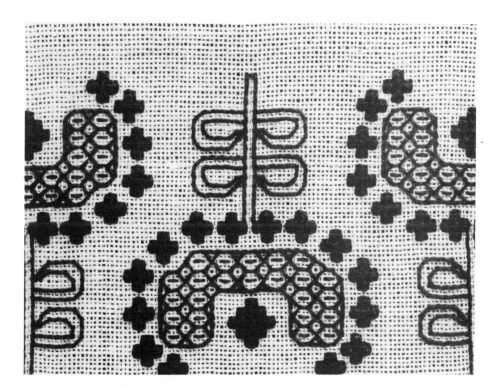

Cut a piece from fabric 43 x 63 cm and mark the centre both ways with a line of basting stitches. The diagram on page 97 gives a complete motif, centre marked by a blank arrow, which should coincide with the widthwise basting stitches. The diagram also shows the arrangement of the stitches on the threads of the fabric represented by the background lines. The layout diagram on this page shows a little more than one quarter of the design, centre indicated by broken lines, which should coincide with the basting stitches. The layout diagram on this page also shows the posi-

tion of the motifs and the number of threads between. With one long side of fabric facing, commence the design centrally 57 threads down and 1 thread to the left of crossed basting stitches and work the lower right-hand quarter following layout diagram. Follow the diagram on page 97 and key for embroidery. All parts similar to numbered parts are worked in the same colour and stitch. Repeat in reverse on to left-hand quarter. Turn fabric and work other half to correspond. Press embroidery on wrong side. To make up, turn back 1.5 cm hems, mitre corners and slipstitch.

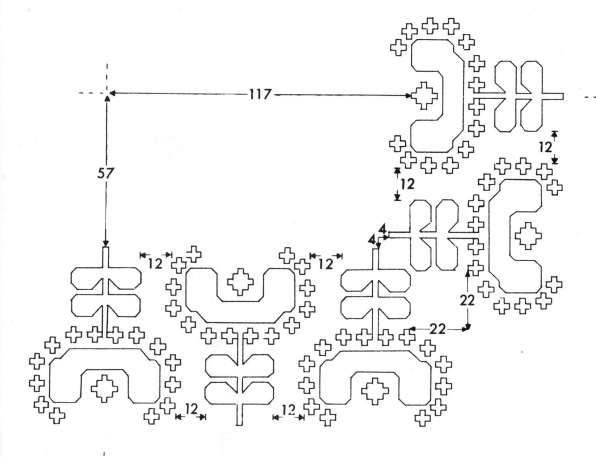

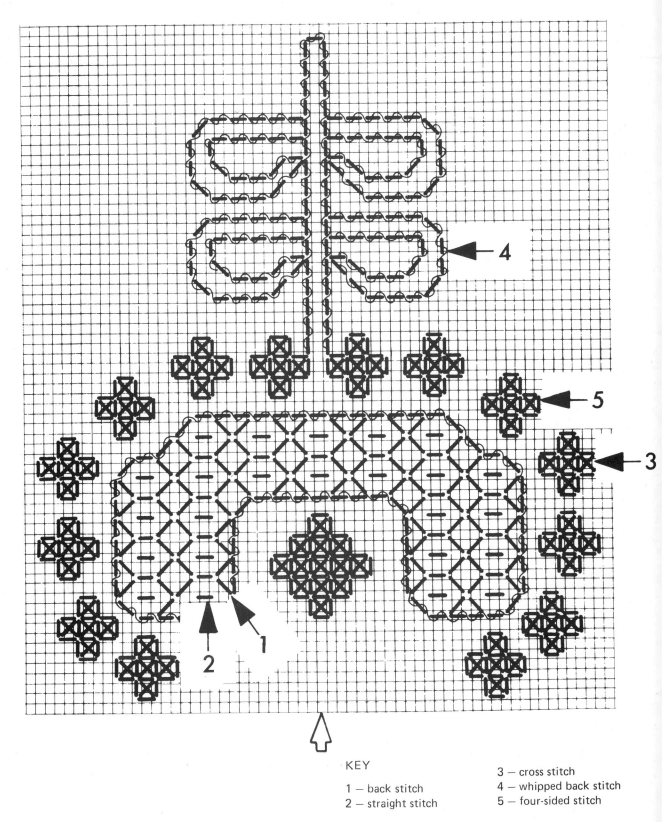

KEY

1 — back stitch

2 — straight stitch

3 — cross stitch

4 — whipped back stitch

5 — four-sided stitch

Tablecloth–Assisi–Italy

Materials
Clark's Anchor Stranded Cotton: 7 skeins Jade 0185;
5 skeins Lido Blue 0410; 3 skeins each Petunia 092,
Cobalt Blue 0134; 2 skeins each Violet 0102, Jade
0188. Use 4 strands throughout.
1.40 m White evenweave embroidery linen, 25 threads
to 2.5 cm, 127 cm (50 in.) wide.
4.20 m Green bobble braid.
Milward International Range tapestry needle No. 24.

Cut a piece from fabric 127 cm square and mark the
centre thread both ways with a line of basting stitches.
The diagram on page 100 gives an eighth of the design
centre indicated by blank arrow which should coincide with the basting stitches. The design is worked
in cross stitch and Holbein stitch over 3 threads of
fabric and it is important that the upper half of all
crosses lie in the same direction. Each background
square on the diagram represents 3 threads of fabric.
Commence the design 139 threads down and 1 thread
to the right at small black arrow and work the section
given. Repeat design in reverse to widthwise basting
stitches to complete lower left-hand quarter of the
design. Work other 3 quarters to correspond. Press
the embroidery on the wrong side. To make up — cut
round edge of tablecloth to make a circle 127 cm in
diameter. Turn to right side 6 mm hem, baste on
braid and stitch.
When using cross stitch combined with Holbein stitch,
all the cross stitches are worked first. It is then
easier to keep the Holbein stitch straight and regular.

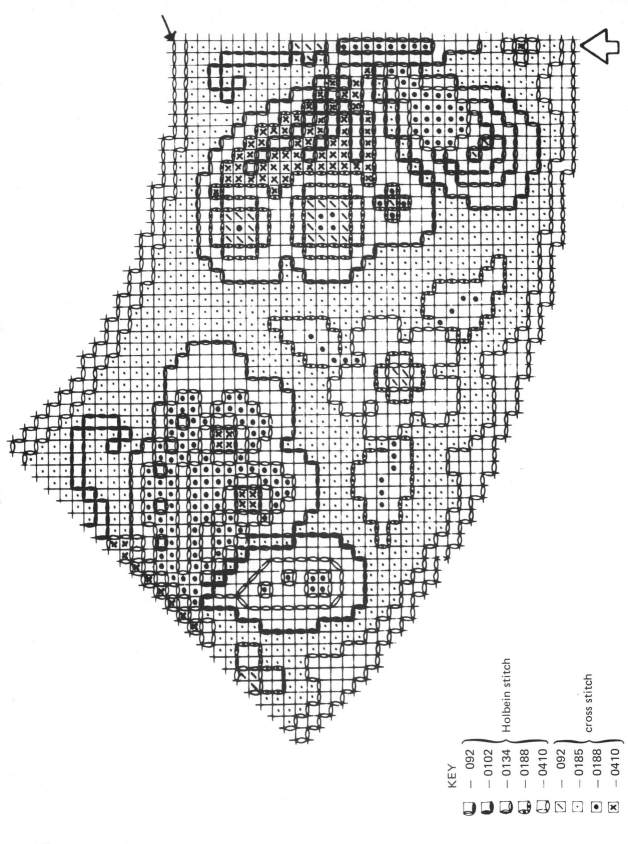

KEY

Holbein stitch
— 092
— 0102
— 0134
— 0188
— 0410

cross stitch
— 092
— 0185
— 0188
— 0410

Cushion cover—free style—Sweden

Materials

Clark's Anchor Stranded Cotton: 11 skeins Peat Brown 0359; 3 skeins Cobalt Blue 0130; 2 skeins Gorse Yellow 0302. Use 6 strands throughout.
40 cm ecru fine embroidery fabric, 112 cm (45 in.) wide.
1.60 m matching fine cord.
Milward International Range crewel needle No. 5.

Cut two pieces from fabric 34.5 x 49.5 cm, fold one piece across the centre both ways and crease lightly. The drawing on page 103 gives half of one motif, centre indicated by broken line. With one long side of fabric facing, trace as given on to lower right-hand quarter, 3 mm down from crossed folds with broken

line on fold. Trace in reverse on to left-hand side of fold to complete one motif. Repeat motif on each side spacing 6 mm apart. Turn fabric and trace other half in same way. Follow the diagram and number key on page 103 for the embroidery. All parts similar to numbered parts are worked in the same colour and stitch. Press the embroidery on the wrong side. To make up, place back and front pieces right sides together and stitch 2 cm from edge on all sides, leaving an opening on one side sufficiently wide to enable a pad to be inserted easily. Press seams and turn to right side. Insert pad. Turn back seam allowance on open edges and slipstitch together. Sew cord in position over seam.

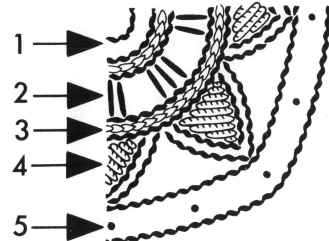

KEY

1 — 0359 — whipped back stitch
2 — 0359 — straight stitch
3 — 0302 — chain stitch
4 — 0130 — satin stitch
5 — 0359 — french knots